Christian Bumper Stickers

Christian Bumper Stickers

A Few Things to Think About

Louise P. Williams

Scriptures taken from:
The New King James Version
And the New International Version

To order additional copies of this book, contact:
Xlibris Corporation
1-888-795-4274
www.Xlibris.com
Orders@Xlibris.com
94907

CONTENTS

Chapter 1 .... *9*

Give God what's right—not what's left. 9
"Pray" is a four-letter word you can say anywhere—
except in public schools. 10
The church is prayer-conditioned. 10
When praying, don't give God instructions—just report for duty. 11
A lot of kneeling will keep you in good standing. 11
He who kneels before God can stand before anyone. 12
Man's way leads to a hopeless end; God's way leads to an endless hope.....13

Chapter 2 .... *14*

To be almost saved is to be totally lost. 14
In the sentence of life, the devil may be a comma—
but never let him be the period...16
Are you wrinkled with burden? Come to the church for a faith-lift........17
We don't change God's message—His message changes us....................18
WARNING: Exposure to the Son may prevent burning.......................19
Plan ahead—It wasn't raining when Noah built the ark. 20
Most people want to serve God, but only in an advisory position.........21

Chapter 3 .... *22*

Wisdom has two parts: having a lot to say; knowing when to say it. 22
Worry is the darkroom in which negatives can develop.....................23
Suffering with truth decay? Brush up on your Bible. 23
Exercise daily—walk with the Lord. 24

God promises a safe landing, not a calm passage................................25
He who angers you controls you..26
Never give the devil a ride! He will always want to drive!—
Give Satan an inch & he'll be a ruler. 27

Chapter 4.. **28**

Read the Bible . . . . It Will Scare The Devil Out of You!.......................28
Be ye fishers of men—you catch them & He'll clean them. 32
God doesn't call the qualified, He qualifies the called:—
When God ordains, He sustains. 33
God doesn't want shares of your life; He wants controlling interest.—
If God is your co-pilot—swap seats! 35
Don't put a question mark where God puts a period. 36

Chapter 5.. **37**

The task ahead of us is never as great as the Power behind us. 37
Forbidden fruits create many jams...38
God grades on the cross, not the curve. 39
Walmart isn't the only saving place! 40
For all you do, His blood's for you!..41
Don't wait for 6 strong men to take you to church. 42

Chapter 6.. **43**

Compassion is difficult to give away because it keeps coming back........43
A family altar can alter a family...44
Too blessed to be depressed/stressed. 45
A clean conscience makes a soft pillow.......................................46
Do your best and then sleep in peace. God is Awake. 47
Nothing else ruins the truth like stretching it. 48
God is good all the time; All the time, God is good..........................49

ACKNOWLEDGEMENTS

I thank God for my grandmother, the late Jimmie G. Brown and mother, the late Edith Powell, for the spiritual upbringing and guidance they provided to me for many years.

I also wish to thank my friend, the late Paul Nix and my sister, Veronica Childers English for sending me emails titled, "Christian Bumper Stickers" and "A Few Things to Think About" respectively.

Louise P. Williams

CHAPTER 1

Give God what's right—not what's left.

Proverbs 3:9, 10—Honor the Lord with your possessions, and with the *first-fruits* of all your increase; so your barns will be filled with plenty, and your vats will overflow with new wine. *Proverbs 23:26*—"My son, give me your heart and let your eyes observe my ways. We can't beat God at giving. *John 3:16*—"For God so loved the world the He gave His only Son that whoever believes in Him should not perish but have everlasting life."

2 Corinthians 8: 1-12—(3) they gave as much as they were able, and even beyond their ability. (5) They gave themselves first to the Lord and then to us in keeping with God's will. Generosity is encouraged! *2 Corinthians 9:6, 7*—Whoever sows sparingly will also reap sparingly, and whoever sows generously will also reap generously; for God loves a cheerful giver. Sow generously! *1 Timothy 6:18*—And to the rich; let them do good that they be rich in good works, ready to give, willing to share. *2 Peter 1:3*—As His divine power has given to us all things that pertain to life and godliness, through the knowledge of Him who called us by glory and virtue.

"Pray" is a four-letter word you can say anywhere—except in public schools.

We can still pray to God anywhere, anytime: in our cars, at the store, in a crowd, in the bathroom, etc. "Men should always pray and not give up . . . ." *Luke 18:1* Pray without ceasing. *1 Thessalonians 5:17*. Do not be anxious about anything, but in everything, by prayer and petition, with thanksgiving, present your request to God. *Philippians 4:6*.

The church is prayer-conditioned.

James 5:13-16—"Is anyone among you suffering? Let him pray. Anyone sick? Let him call for the elders of the church. The prayer of faith will save the sick. Confess your faults to one another, that you might be healed. The effective, fervent prayer of a righteous man avails much. *Romans 12:12*—rejoicing in hope, patient in tribulation, continuing steadfastly in prayer.

When praying, don't give God instructions—just report for duty.

Philippians 4:6—When praying, do give God praise, adoration, honor, supplication with thanksgiving. *Hebrews 13:15*—"Therefore by Him let us continually offer the sacrifice of praise to God, that is, the fruit of our lips, giving thanks to His name."

We don't give Him instructions:

Matthew. 17:5, 6; Acts 7:37; Deuteronomy 18:15, 19—God said, "This is My Beloved Son, in whom I'm well pleased, hear Him." *Matthew. 28:18*—Jesus Himself said, "All authority has been given to me . . . ."

Just report for duty: *Matthew 28:19, 20*—"Go make disciples of all nations, baptizing them in the name of the Father and of the Son and of the Holy Spirit, and teaching them to obey everything I have commanded you."

Hebrews 10:24, 25 "And let us consider how we may encourage one another on toward love and good deeds. Let us not give up meeting (assembling) together, as some are in the habit of doing, but let us encourage one another . . . ." Assemble with other Christians (church, Body of Christ) to worship and commune; depart for duty, service, to share the message.

A lot of kneeling will keep you in good standing.

1 Thessalonians. 5:17—"Pray without ceasing. "We shall all stand before the judgment seat of Christ; every knee shall bow to Me." *Romans 14:10,11*; *1 Corinthians 16:13*—"Be on your guard, stand firm in the faith . . . ." *Philippians 3:17*—"Join with others in following my example, brothers, and take note of those who live according to the pattern we gave you." *Philippians 4:1*—"Therefore my brothers, you whom I love an long for, my joy and crown, ... stand firm in the Lord, dear friends!"

He who kneels before God can stand before anyone.

Ephesians 6:11-18—(11) Put on the whole armor of God, that you may be able to stand against the wiles of the devil. (13) "Therefore put on the full armor of God, so that when the day of evil comes, you may be able to stand your ground, and after you have done everything, to stand. Stand firm then, with the belt of truth . . . ." (18) And pray in the Spirit on all occasions . . . ."

Man's way leads to a hopeless end; God's way leads to an endless hope.

Regarding man's way: *Proverbs 14:12*—"There is a *way* that seems right to man, but its end is the *way* of death." *Psalm 67:1, 2*—That your *way* may be known on earth . . . . *Psalm 119:104*—"Therefore I hate every false way . . . ." *Psalm 139:23, 24*—"Search me O God, and know my heart; try me and know my anxieties; and see if there is any wicked *way* in me and lead me in the *way* everlasting."

Regarding God's Way: *Matthew 7:13, 14; 21-23*—"Enter by the narrow gate, for wide is the gate and broad is the way that leads to destruction," "Because narrow is the gate and difficult is the *way* which leads to life, and there are few who find it." (21) "Not everyone who says to Me, 'Lord, Lord,' shall enter the kingdom of heaven, but he who does the will of My Father in heaven." *Matthew 15:1-9*—"in vain do they worship Me, teaching as doctrines the commandments of men . . . ." *Matthew 22:16*—"Teacher we know that You are true, and teach the *way* of God in truth . . . ." *John 14:6*—Jesus said, "I am the *way*, the truth, and the life. No man comes to the Father except through Me. *Acts 18:26*—When Aquila and Priscilla heard him (Apollo's) they took him aside and explained to him the *way* of God more accurately.

CHAPTER 2

To be almost saved is to be totally lost.

Acts 26:27-29—"King Agrippa, do you believe the prophets? I know that you believe."

(28) Then Agrippa said to Paul, "You almost persuaded me to become a Christian."

(29) And Paul said, "I would to God that not only you, but also all who hear me today, might become both almost and altogether such as I am . . . . *John 12:42,43*—Nevertheless even among the rulers many believed in Him, but because of the Pharisees they did not confess Him, lest they should be put out of the synagogue. (43) For they loved the praise of men more than the praise of God. *Acts 5:29-32*—"We ought to obey God rather than men." (32) "And we are His witnesses to these things, and so also is the Holy Spirit whom God has given to those who obey Him. *Luke 6:46*—"But why do you call Me Lord, Lord and do not do the things which I say?" *Luke 8:12*—Those by the way side are they that hear; then comes the devil and takes away the word out of their hearts, lest they should believe and be saved. *James 2:14-26*—(19) You believe that there is one God. You do well. Even the demons believe and tremble. *2 Peter 1:10*—make your calling and election sure.

2 Peter 3:9—The Lord is not slack concerning His promise—but is longsuffering toward us, not willing that any should perish but that all should come to repentance.

1 John 2:3-5—Now by this we know that we know Him, if we keep His commandments. (4) He who says, "I know Him," and does not keep His commandments, is a liar, and the truth is not in him.

In the sentence of life, the devil may be a comma—but never let him be the period.

Luke 5:32—I came not to call the righteous, but sinners to repentance. *[Matt. 9:13; Mark 2:1] John 8:31-34*—(32) You will know the truth, and the truth shall set you free."

(34) Jesus said, "I tell you the truth, everyone who sins, is a slave to sin.

Acts 2:38—"Repent and be baptized for the remission/forgiveness of your sins . . . . " *[Acts 3:19; 5:31; 8:2])* *Acts 17:30*—In the past God overlooked ignorance, but now commands all people everywhere to repent. *Acts 26:20*—repent and turn to God and perform deeds worthy of repentance. *Romans 3:23*—For all have sinned and fall short of the glory of God. *Romans 5:6, 8,9,19* (8) while we were yet sinners, Christ died for us. *2 Peter 3:9*—The Lord is not slack concerning his promise . . . . but is longsuffering toward us, not willing that any should perish, but that all should come to repentance. *Romans 2:4*—God's kindness is meant to lead you to repentance. *2 Corinthians 7:9, 10*—(10) Godly sorrow brings repentance that leads to salvation . . . . but worldly sorrow brings death.

Are you wrinkled with burden? Come to the church for a faith-lift.

Matthew 11:28-30—"Come to me all you who are weary and burdened, and I will give you rest. (29) Take my yoke upon you and learn from me, (30) for my yoke is easy and my burden is light. *Galatians 6:2-10*—(2) Bear one another's burdens and so fulfill the law of Christ. (9) Let us not become weary in doing good, for at the proper time, we will reap a harvest if we do not give up. *Ephesians 5:27*—that He might present it to himself a glorious church, not having spot or wrinkle, or any such thing; but that it should be holy and without blemish. *Acts 6:7*—And the word of God increased. The number of disciples in Jerusalem increased rapidly and a large number of priests became obedient to the faith. *Acts 14:27*—They gathered the church together and reported all that God had done through them and how he had opened the door of faith, and increased in number daily.

Acts 26:18—Jesus sends Paul to "open their eyes, and turn them from darkness to light, and from the power of Satan unto God, that they may receive forgiveness of sins, and an inheritance among them which are sanctified by faith that was also in him."

2 Corinthian 13:5—Examine yourself, whether you are in the faith.

We don't change God's message—His message changes us.

Acts 2:29-47—(31) seeing what was ahead, he spoke of the resurrection of Christ. (37) When the people heard this, they were cut to the heart and said to Peter and the other apostles, "Brothers, what shall we do?" (38) Peter replied, "Repent and be baptized every one of you, in the name of Jesus Christ for the forgiveness/remission of your sins. And you will receive the gift of the Holy Spirit. (41) Those who accepted his message were baptized, and about three thousand were added unto them. *[Matt 28:19-20; Mark 16:15, 16; Luke 24:46, 47]*

Acts 8:12—But when they believed Phillip preaching the things concerning the kingdom of God, and the name of Jesus Christ, they were baptized, both men and women.

Acts 18:8—And Crispus, the chief ruler of the synagogue, believed on the Lord with his entire house, and many Corinthians hearing, believed and were baptized. *Acts 19:5*—when they heard this, they were baptized in the name of the Lord Jesus. *Romans 6:3*—Know you not, that so many of us were baptized into Jesus Christ were baptized into his death?

Galatians 3:27—For as many of you as have been baptized into Christ have put on Christ. *Luke 7:30*—But the Pharisees and lawyers rejected the counsel of God against themselves, being not baptized.

WARNING: Exposure to the Son may prevent burning.

Matthew 18:11—"For the Son of Man has come to save that which is lost." *[Luke 19:10]*

Luke 9:56—"For the Son of Man did not come to destroy men's lives but to save them.

John 3:1-21—(3) Jesus said, "I tell you the truth, no one can **see** the kingdom of God unless he is born again. (5) I tell you the truth; no one can **enter** the kingdom of God unless he is born of water and the Spirit. (7) You must be born again." (17) "For God did not send His Son into the world to condemn the world, but that the world through Him might be saved."

John 3:36—He who believes in the Son has everlasting life, he who does not believe the Son shall not see life, but the wrath of God abides on him. *[John 5:24-30; John 6:40; 1John 5:11, 12]* *John 8:36*—"Therefore if the Son makes you free, you shall be free indeed." *Acts 8:35-38*—(37) Then Peter said, "If you believe with all your heart, you may (*be baptized*)." And he answered and said, "I believe that Jesus Christ is the Son of God." *Hebrews 4:14*—Seeing then that we have a great High Priest who has passed through the heavens, Jesus the Son of God, let us hold fast our confession. *1 John 4:15*—Whoever confesses that Jesus is the Son of God; God abides in him, and he in God.

2 John 1:9—Whoever transgresses and does not abide in the doctrine of Christ does not have God. He who abides in the doctrine of Christ has both the Father and the Son.

Plan ahead—It wasn't raining when Noah built the ark.

Hebrews 11: 1-31—(1) Now faith is the substance of things hoped for, the evidence of things not seen. (6) But without faith, it is impossible to please Him, for he who comes to God must believe that He is, and that he is a rewarder of those who earnestly seek Him.

(7) By faith Noah, being divinely warned of things not yet seen, **moved** with Godly fear, **prepared** an ark for the saving of his household. *Romans 10:14-17*—How then shall they call on Him in whom they have not believed? And how shall they believe in Him of whom they have not heard? And how shall they hear without a preacher? And how shall they preach unless they are sent? As it is written: "How beautiful are the feet of those who preach the gospel of peace, (16) But they have not all obeyed the gospel. (17) So then faith comes by hearing, and hearing by the word of God. *1 Corinthians 2:5*—That your faith should not stand in the wisdom of men, but in the power of God.

1 Corinthians 16:13—Watch ye, stand fast in the faith. *Galatians 3:14*—The blessing of Abraham might come on the Gentiles through Jesus Christ, that we might receive the promise of the Spirit through faith. *Galatians 3:22*—But the scripture hath concluded all under sin, that the promise by faith of Jesus Christ might be given to them that believe.

2 Thessalonians 3:2—for not everyone has faith. *2 Timothy 1:13*—Hold fast the form of sound doctrine, which you heard of me in faith and love which is in Christ Jesus.
[2 Thess. 1:6-10].

Most people want to serve God, but only in an advisory position.

Matthew 9:24—"A disciple is not above his teacher, nor a servant above his master." *Matthew 16:24*—"If anyone desires to come after Me, let him deny himself and take up his cross, and follow Me. *Matthew17:5*—God said, "This is My beloved Son, in whom I am well pleased. Hear Him!" *Matthew 20:26-28*—Whoever desires to become great among you, let him be your servant. And whoever desires to be first among you, let him be your slave. Just as the Son of Man did not come to be served but to serve, and to give His life a ransom for many. *John 12:26*—"If anyone serves Me, let him follow Me; and where I am, there My servant will be also. If anyone serves Me, him My Father will honor."

John 13:15-17—Jesus said, "For I have given you an example, that you should do as I have done to you. (16) A servant is not greater than his master; (17) if you know these things, happy are you if you do them." *John 15:20*—"A servant is not greater than his master."

CHAPTER 3

Wisdom has two parts: having a lot to say; knowing when to say it.

Proverbs 3:13—Happy is the man who finds wisdom and the man who gains understanding.

Proverbs 4:7—Wisdom is the principal thing; therefore get wisdom. And in all your getting, get understanding. *Proverbs 9:10*—The fear of the Lord is the beginning of wisdom and the knowledge of the Holy One is understanding. *1 Corinthians 4:5*—Walk in wisdom toward them that are without, redeeming the time. [*Eph.5:15, 16*] *1 Corinthians 2:5*—That your faith should not stand in the wisdom of men, but in the power of God.

1 Corinthians 3:18, 19—(19) for the wisdom of this world is foolishness with God.

James 1:5, 6—If any of you lacks wisdom, let him ask of God, who gives to all liberally and without reproach, and it will be given to him. (6) But let him ask in faith, with no doubting, for he who doubts is like a wave of the sea driven and tossed by the wind. *James 3:13-18*—(13) Who is wise and understanding among you? Let him show by good conduct that his works are done in the meekness of wisdom. (17) But the wisdom that is from above is first pure, then peaceable, gentle, willing to yield, full of mercy and good fruits, without partiality and without hypocrisy.

Worry is the darkroom in which negatives can develop.

Matthew 6:25-34—Do not worry about your life, what you will eat or drink; or about your body, what you will wear. (27) Who of you by worrying can add a single hour to his life?

(33) But seek ye first the kingdom and His righteousness, and all these things will be given to you as well. (34) Therefore, do not worry about tomorrow, for tomorrow will worry about itself. Each day has enough trouble of its' own. *Philippians 4:6-9*—Do not be anxious about anything, but in everything, by prayer and petition with thanksgiving, present your requests to God. (7) And the peace of God, which transcends all understanding, will guard your hearts and minds in Christ Jesus. (8) Finally brothers, whatever is true, whatever is noble, whatever is right, whatever is pure, whatever is lovely, whatever is admirable, if anything is excellent or praiseworthy; think about such things.

Suffering with truth decay? Brush up on your Bible.

John 8:30-32—As he spoke these words, many believed Him. "If you abide in My word, you are My disciples indeed. "And you shall know the *truth*, and the *truth* shall make you free." *John 14:16*—Jesus said to them, "I am the way, the *truth* and the life. No one comes to the Father except through Me." *2 Timothy 2:15*—Be diligent (study) to present yourself approved to God, a worker who does not need to be ashamed, rightly dividing the word of truth. *1 Peter 3:15*—But in your hearts set apart Christ as Lord. Always be prepared to give an answer to everyone who asks you to give the reason for the hope that you have. But do this with gentleness and respect.

Exercise daily—walk with the Lord.

Galatians 5:25—If we live in the Spirit, let us also *walk* in the Spirit. *1 John 1:7*—But if we *walk* in the light as He is in the light, we have fellowship with one another, and the blood of Jesus Christ cleanses us from all sin. (6) If we say that we have fellowship with Him and walk in darkness, we lie and do not practice the truth. *1 John 2:3-6*—We know that we have come to know him if we obey his commands. (4) The man who says, "I know him," but does not do what he commands is a liar, and the truth is not in him. (5) But if anyone obeys his word, God's love is truly made complete in him. This is how we know we are in him.

(6) Whoever claims to live in him must *walk* as Jesus did.

God promises a safe landing, not a calm passage.

Matthew 5:10-12—Blessed are those who are persecuted because of righteousness, for theirs is the kingdom of heaven. Blessed are you when people insult you, persecute you and falsely say all kinds of evil against you because of Me. Rejoice and be exceedingly glad, because great is your reward in heaven, for in the same way they persecuted the prophets who were before you. *Acts 14:22*—strengthening the souls of the disciples, exhorting them to continue in the faith, and saying, "We must through many tribulations enter the kingdom of God.

2 Thessalonians 1:4, 5—Therefore, among God's churches we boast about your persecutions and trials you are enduring. All this is evidence that God's judgment is right, and as a result you will be counted worthy of the kingdom of God, for which you are suffering.

Philippians 1:29—For to you it has been granted on behalf of Christ, not only to believe in Him, but also to suffer for His sake. *Romans 8:17, 18*—and if children, then heirs; heirs of God and joint heirs with Christ, if indeed we suffer with Him, that we may also be glorified together. (18) For I consider that the sufferings of this present time are not worthy to be compared with the glory which shall be revealed in us. *Romans 8:35-37*—Who shall separate us from the love of Christ? Shall tribulations, or distress, or persecution, or famine, or nakedness, or peril, or sword? (37) Yet in all these things we are more than conquerors through Him who loved us. *2 Timothy 2:11, 12*—This is a faithful saying: For if we die with Him, we shall also live with Him. (12) If we endure, we shall also reign with Him! *2 Timothy 3:12*—All who desire to live godly in Christ Jesus will suffer persecution.

James 1:2-4, 12—Consider it pure joy, my brothers, whenever you face trials of many kinds, because you know that the testing of your faith develops perseverance. Perseverance must finish its work so that you may be mature and complete, not lacking anything. (12) Blessed is the man who perseveres under trial, because when he has stood the test, he will receive the crown of life that God has promised to those who love Him. *2 John 4:8*—Watch out that you do not lose what you have worked for, but that you may be rewarded fully.

He who angers you controls you.

Ephesians 4:26-32—"In your anger do not sin." And do not let the sun go down while you are still angry, and do not give the devil a foothold (opportunity). (29) Do not let any unwholesome talk come out of your mouths, but what is helpful for building others up according to their needs, that it may benefit those who listen. (31) Get rid of all bitterness, rage and anger, brawling and slander, along with every form of malice. (32) Be kind and compassionate to one another, forgiving each other, just as in Christ, God forgave you.

Colossians 3:8—But now ye also put off these: anger, wrath, malice, blasphemy, filthy communication out of your mouth. *John 8:44*—You are of your father the devil, and the lusts of your father you will do. He was a murder from the beginning, and abode not in the truth, because there is no truth in him. When he speaks a lie, he speaks of his own: for he is a liar and the father of it.

Ephesians 4:27—Neither give place to the devil. *Ephesians 6:11*—Put on the whole armor of God, that you may be able to stand against the wiles of the devil. *2 Timothy 2:22-26*—Flee the evil desire of youth, and pursue righteousness, faith, love and peace . . . . And the Lord's servant must not quarrel; instead, he must be kind to everyone, able to teach, not resentful. Those who oppose him he must gently instruct, in hope that God will grant them repentance leading them to a knowledge of the truth, and that they will come to their senses and escape from the trap of the devil, who has taken them captive to do his will. *James 4:7-10*—Submit yourself, then to God. Resist the devil, and he will flee from you. (8) Come near to God and he will come near to you. (10) Humble yourself before the Lord and He will lift you up.

1 Peter 5:8—Be self-controlled and alert. Your enemy the devil prowls around like a roaring lion looking for someone to devour. *1 John 3:8*—He who does what is sinful is the devil, because the devil has been sinning from the beginning. The reason the Son of God appeared was to destroy the devil's work.

Never give the devil a ride! He will always want to drive!—Give Satan an inch & he'll be a ruler.

Genesis 3—The serpent was more cunning than any beast of the field which the Lord God had made. (4) And the serpent said to the woman, "You will not surely die." (5) "For God knows that in the day you eat of it (fruit from tree of knowledge) your eyes will be opened, and you will be like God, knowing good and evil." *Matthew 4:1-11*—Then Jesus was led by the Spirit into the desert to be tempted by the devil. (3) . . . ."If you are the Son of God, command that these stones become bread." (6) . . . . "If you are the Son of God, throw yourself down." (9) . . . . "All these things I will give you if you worship me." (10) Jesus said, "Away with you Satan, for it is written, you shall worship the Lord your God, and Him only you shall serve." *[Luke 4:8] Matthew 16:23*—Jesus said, "Get behind Me "Satan! You are a stumbling block to me; you do not have in mind the things of God, but things of men." *Ephesians 4:27*—do not give the devil a foothold (opportunity). *Ephesians 6:11*—Put on the whole armor of God, that you may be able to stand against the wiles of the devil. *2 Thessalonians 2:1-12*—(9) The coming of the lawless one will be in accordance with the work of Satan with all power, miracles, signs and wonders. (10) And with all unrighteous deception among those who perish, because they did not receive the love of truth that they might be saved. *1 Timothy 5:14, 15*— . . . give no opportunity to the adversary to speak reproachfully. For some have already turned aside after Satan. *2 Timothy 2:26*—And that they may come to their senses and escape the snare of the devil, having been taken captive by him to do his will. *James 1:13-16*—Let no one say when he is tempted, "I am tempted by God;" (14) but each one is tempted when he is drawn away by his own desires and enticed. (15) When desire is conceived, it gives birth to sin; and sin, when it is full-grown, brings forth death. *[Gen. 3]* (16) Do not be deceived, my beloved brothers. *1 Peter 5:8, 9*—Be sober; be vigilant; because your adversary the devil walks about like a roaring lion, seeking whom he may devour. Resist him, steadfast in the faith, knowing that the same sufferings are experienced by your brotherhood in the world.

1 John 3:8—He who sins is of the devil. *Revelation 12:9*—The great dragon was cast down; that ancient serpent called the devil, or Satan, who leads (deceives) the whole world; he was cast to the earth, and his angels were cast with him.

CHAPTER 4

Read the Bible . . . . It Will Scare The Devil Out of You!

Life is short. *Death* is certain. *Judgment* is promised. *Eternity* is long.

Job 14:1, 2—Man who is born of woman is of few days and full of trouble. He comes forth Like a flower and fades away; He flees like a shadow and does not continue.

Ecclesiastes 3:1, 2—To everything there is a season. A time for every purpose under heaven: A time to be born, and a time to die. *Ecclesiastes 9:5, 10*—For the living know that they will die; but the dead knows nothing and they have no more reward. (10) Whatever your hands find to do, do it with your might; for there is no work or device or knowledge or wisdom in the grave where you are going. *Ecclesiastes 12:1, 7, 13, 14*—(1) Remember now your Creator in the days of your youth, before the difficult days come and the years draw near . . . . (7) Then the dust will return to the earth as it was, and the spirit will return to God who gave it. [*See Luke 16:19-31; Acts 2:27 regarding the soul.*] (13) Fear God and keep His commandments, for this is the whole duty of man. (14) For God will bring every work into judgment. Including every secret thing, whether it is good, or whether it is evil.

Matthew 7:21—Not everyone who says to me, Lord, Lord, will enter the kingdom of heaven, but only he who does the will of my father who is in heaven. (23) Then I will tell them plainly, "I never knew you. Away from me, you evildoers." *John 5:25-30*—" . . . . the time is coming and has now come when the dead will hear the voice of the Son of God and those who hear will live. (27) And He has given Him authority to judge because He is the Son of God. (28) "Do not be amazed at this, for a time is coming when all who are in their graves will hear his voice (29) and come out; those who have done good will rise to live, and those who have done evil will rise to be condemned [*Matt. 25:31-46*]. *Luke 13:3*—I tell you no. But unless you repent, you will all likewise perish. *Act 17:30, 31*—In the past God overlooked such ignorance, but now he commands all people everywhere to repent. For He has set a day when He will judge the world with justice by the man he has appointed. He has given proof of this to all men by raising Him from the dead (Jesus Christ).

2 Corinthians 5:10,11—For we must all appear before the judgment seat of Christ, that each one may receive the things done in the body, according to what he has done, whether good or bad. Knowing therefore, the terror of the Lord, we persuade men.

1 Thessalonians 4:16,17—For the Lord himself will come down from heaven, with a loud command, with the voice of the archangel and with the trumpet call of God, and the dead **"in"** Christ will rise first. After that, we who are still alive and are left will be caught up together with them in the clouds to meet the Lord in the air. Are you **"in"** Christ? [*see Romans 6:3-5; Galatians 3:26, 27*] *2 Thessalonians 1:6-10*—since it is a righteous thing with God to repay tribulation to those who trouble you, and to give you who are troubled rest with us when the Lord Jesus is revealed from heaven with His mighty angels, in flaming fire taking vengeance on those who do not know God and on those who **do not obey** the gospel of our Lord Jesus Christ. These shall be punished with everlasting destruction from the presence of the Lord and from the glory of His power [*Matt. 24:29-44*]. Have you **obeyed** the gospel message?

Read the Bible . . . . cont.

*[See Matt. 28:19, 20; Mark 16:15, 16; Luke 24:46-49; Acts 2:36:39]
Hebrews 2:2, 3*—For if the message spoken by angels was binding, and every violation and disobedience received its just punishment, (3) how shall we escape if we ignore such a great salvation?

Hebrews 9:27—And it is appointed for men to die once, but after this the judgment.

James 4:14—Whereas you do not know what will happen tomorrow. For what is your life? It is even a vapor that appears for a little time and then vanishes away. *1 Peter 1:17-19*—And if you call on the Father, who without partiality judges according to each one's work, conduct yourselves throughout the time of your sojourning here in fear; knowing that you were not redeemed with corruptible things . . . . (19) but with the precious blood of Christ, as of a lamb without blemish and without spot. *2 Peter 3:9,10*—The Lord is not slack concerning His promise, as some count slackness, but is longsuffering toward us, not willing that any should perish but that all should come to repentance. But the day of the Lord will come as a thief in the night, in which the heavens will pass away with a great noise, and the elements will melt with fervent heat; both the earth and the works that are in it will be burned up. Therefore, since all these things will be dissolved, what manner of persons ought you to be in holy conduct and godliness? *Jude 14-16*—"See, the Lord is coming with thousands upon thousands of His holy ones to judge everyone, and to convict all the ungodly of all the ungodly acts they have done in the ungodly way, and of all the harsh words ungodly sinners have spoken against Him. *Revelation 14:6, 7, 13*—Then I saw another angel flying in mid air, and he had the eternal gospel to proclaim to those who live on the earth; to every nation, tribe, language and people. "Fear God and give Him glory, because the hour of His judgment has come." (13) " . . . . Blessed are the dead who die **"in"** the Lord from now on; they will rest from their labor, for their deeds will follow them." *Revelation 20:12-15*—And I saw the dead, great and small, standing before the throne, and books were opened. Another book was opened, which is the book of life. The dead were judged according to what they had done as recorded in the books. The sea gave up the dead that were in it, and death and Hades gave up the dead that were in them, each person was judged according to what he had done. Then death and Hades was throne into the lake of fire. The lake of fire is the second death. If anyone's name was not found written in the book of life, he was thrown into the lake of fire.

Revelation 21:8, 27—But the cowardly, the unbelieving, the vile, the murderers, the sexually immoral, those who practice magic arts, the idolaters and all liars; their place will be in the fiery lake. This is the second death. (27) Nothing impure will ever enter it, (The New Jerusalem) nor will anyone who does what is shameful or deceitful, but only those whose names are written in the Lamb's book of life. *Rev. 22:12-15*—" . . . . My reward is with Me, and I will give to everyone according to what he has done." (14) Blessed are those who do His commandments, that they may have the right to the tree of life . . . (15) But outside are dogs and those who practice magic arts, sexually immoral, murderers, idolaters and everyone who loves and practices a lie.

Be ye fishers of men—you catch them & He'll clean them.

Proverbs 11:30– . . . . And he who wins souls is wise. *Matthew 4:18-25*—(19) And He said to them, "Follow Me, and I will make you fishers of men." (20) Then they immediately left their nets and followed Him. (21) . . . . And He called them, (22) and immediately they left the boat and their father, and followed Him. (23) Now Jesus went about all Galilee *teaching* the gospel of the kingdom . . . . (25) And great multitudes followed Him . . . .

Matthew 8:9— . . . He saw a man named Matthew sitting at the tax office and He said to him, "Follow Me." And he rose and followed Him. *Matthew 9:37, 37*—He said to His disciples, "The harvest is plentiful, but the laborers are few. Therefore, pray the Lord of harvest to send out laborers into His harvest." *John 15:5-8*—I am the vine; you are the branches. If a man remains in me and I in him, he will bear much fruit; apart from Me you can do nothing. If anyone does not remain in me, he is like a branch that is thrown away and withers; such branches are picked up, thrown into the fire and burned. If you remain in Me and my words remain in you, ask whatever you wish, and it will be given you. This is to my Father's glory, that you bear much fruit, showing yourselves to be my disciples.

God doesn't call the qualified, He qualifies the called:—When God ordains, He sustains.

Matthew 5:1-12—And seeing the multitude, He went up on a mountain, and when was seated His disciples came to Him. Then He opened His mouth and *taught* them . . . . (Beatitudes). *Matthew 15:15, 16*—I no longer call you servants, because a servant doesn't know his master's business. Instead, I have called you friends, for everything that I have learned from my Father, I have made known to you. You did not choose me, but I chose you and appointed you to go and bear fruit; fruit that will last. *Matthew 16:7, 8, 13*—But I tell you the truth: It is good that I am going away. Unless I go away, the Counselor will not come to you; but if I go, I will send Him to you. When he comes, he will convict the world of guilt in regard to sin and righteousness and judgement. (13) But when he, the Spirit of truth comes, he will guide you into all truth. *Matthew 20:16*—So the last will be first, and the first will be last. For many are called, but few are chosen. *Acts 2:38, 39*—"Repent and be baptized every one of you, in the name of Jesus Christ for the remission/forgiveness of your sins. And you will receive the gift of the Holy Spirit. The promise is for your and your children and for all who are far off: for all whom the Lord our God will call." *Romans 3:23,24*—For all have sinned and fall short of the glory of God, and are justified freely by His grace through the redemption that came by Christ Jesus. *Romans 8:28*—And we know that in all things God works for the good of those who love Him, who have been called according to His purpose. *1 Corinthians 7:17*—But as God has distributed to each one, as the Lord has called each one, so let him walk. And so I ordain in all the churches. *2 Timothy 1:8, 9*—Paul said, "Do not be ashamed to testify about our Lord, or ashamed of me his prisoner. But join with me in suffering for the gospel, by the power of God, (9) who has saved us and called us to a holy life: not because of anything we have done, but because of His own purpose and grace. *1 Peter 2:9*—But you are a chosen people, a royal priesthood, a holy nation, a people belonging to God, that you may declare the praises of Him who called you out of darkness into His wonderful light. *2 Peter 1:3, 4-11*—His divine power has given us everything we need for life and godliness through our knowledge of Him who called us by His own glory and goodness. (4) Through these he has given us His very great

And precious promises, so that through them you may participate in the divine nature and escape the corruption in the world caused by evil desires. (10) Therefore, my brothers, be all the more eager to make your calling and election sure. For if you do these things, you will never fall, (11) and you will receive a rich welcome into the eternal kingdom of our Lord and Savior Jesus Christ. *Revelation 2:10* – . . . . Be faithful, even to the point of death, and I will give you the crown of life.

God doesn't want shares of your life; He wants controlling interest.—If God is your co-pilot—swap seats!

Exodus 20:5—. . . . For I, the Lord your God, am a jealous God. *Deuteronomy 4:24*—For the Lord your God is a consuming fire, a jealous God. *Ecclesiastes 12:13*—Fear God and keep His commandments, for this is the whole duty of man. *Matthew 10: 27, 28*—Jesus said, "What I tell you in the dark, speak in the daylight; what is whispered in your ear, proclaim from the roofs. Do not be afraid of those who kill the body but cannot kill the soul. Rather, be afraid of the One who can destroy both soul and body in hell." *Luke 9:23*—Jesus said, "If anyone desires to come after me, let him deny himself, and take up his cross daily and follow me [*Matt. 16:24, 25; Mark 8:34, 35*]. *Romans 12:1, 2*— . . . . Present your bodies a living sacrifice, holy, acceptable to God, which is your reasonable service. And do not be conformed to this world, but be transformed by the renewing of your mind, that you may prove what is the good and acceptable and perfect will of God. *2 Corinthians 11:2, 3*—The Apostle Paul said, "For I am jealous for you with godly jealousy. For I have betrothed you to one husband, that I may present you as a chaste virgin to Christ. But I fear, lest somehow, as the serpent deceived Eve by his craftiness, so your minds may be corrupted from the simplicity that is in Christ."

Don't put a question mark where God puts a period.

Matthew 17:5, 6—While he was still speaking, a bright cloud enveloped them, and a voice from the cloud said, "This is My Son, in whom I love; with Him I am well pleased. Listen to Him!" When the disciples heard this, they fell face down to the ground, terrified.

Matthew 28:18—Then Jesus came to them and said, "All authority in heaven and in earth has been given to me." *Mark 4: 39-41*—And He arose, and rebuked the wind and said unto the sea, "Peace be still." And the wind ceased, and there was a great calm. (41) And they feared exceedingly and said to one another, what manner of man is this that even the wind and sea obey Him [*see Matt. 8:25-27*]. *John 1:1, 2*—In the beginning was the Word, and the Word was with God, and the Word was God. He was with God in the beginning [*see Gen. 1:26*]. *John 8:58*—Jesus said unto them, "Verily, verily, I say unto you, Before Abraham was, I AM." *John 10:15-18*—(18) No man takes it (life) from me, but I lay it down myself. I have power to lay it down, and I have power to take it again. This commandment I have received of My Father. *Revelation 1:8*—"I am the Alpha and the Omega," says the Lord God, "who is, and was, and who is to come, the Almighty." *Revelation 22:13*—"I am the Alpha and the Omega, the First and the Last, the Beginning and the End."

CHAPTER 5

The task ahead of us is never as great as the Power behind us.

Matthew 11:28-30—"Come to me, all you who labor and are heavy laden and I will give you rest. Take my yoke upon you and learn from me, for I am gentle and lowly in heart, and you will find rest for your souls. For my yoke is easy and my burden is light."

Romans 16:20—And the God of peace will crush Satan under your feet shortly.

1 Corinthians 10:13—No temptation has overtaken you except such as is common to man; but God is faithful, who will not allow you to be tempted beyond what you are able, but with the temptation, will also make the way of escape, that you may be able to bear it.

2 Corinthians 12:9, 10—But He said to me, "My grace is sufficient for you, for my power is made perfect in weakness." Therefore I will boast all the more gladly about my weaknesses, so that Christ's power may rest on me. That's why for Christ's sake, I delight in weaknesses, in insults, in hardships, in persecutions, in difficulties. For when I am weak, then I am strong. *1 Timothy 1:7*—For God has not given us a spirit of fear, but of power and of love and of a sound mind. *1 John 4:4*—You are of God dear children, and have overcome them, because He who is in you is greater than he who is in the world!

Forbidden fruits create many jams.

Genesis 3—(2) And the woman said to the serpent, "We may eat the fruit of the trees of the garden; (3)but of the fruit of that which is in the midst of the garden, God has said 'You shall not eat, nor shall you touch it, lest you die". (12) Then the man said, "The woman whom you gave to be with me, she gave me of the tree, and I ate." (13) . . . . .And the woman said, "The serpent deceived me and I ate." (14) The Lord God said to the serpent: (16) to the woman He said: (17) Then to Adam He said:

Matthew 7:16, 17—You will know them by their fruit. "Even so, every good tree bears good fruit, but a bad tree bears bad fruit." *Galatians 5:22, 23*—But the fruit of the Spirit is love, joy, peace, patience, kindness, goodness, faithfulness, (23) gentleness and self-control. Against such things there is no law. *Colossians 1:10*—that you may have a walk worthy of the Lord, fully pleasing Him, being fruitful in every good work and increasing in the knowledge of God. *John 5:8*—"By this My Father is glorified, that you bear much fruit; so you will be my disciples." *Romans 7:4*—so my brothers, you also died to the law through the body of Christ, that you might belong to another, to Him who was raised from the dead, in order that we might bear fruit to God. *James 3:18*—Now the fruit of righteousness is sown in peace by those who make peace.

God grades on the cross, not the curve.

Matthew 16:24—Then Jesus said to His disciples, "If anyone desires to come after me, let him deny himself, take up his cross and follow Me." *Matthew 27:40, 50-54*—"You, who destroy the temple and build it in three days, save yourself! Come down from the cross, if you are the Son of God!" (50) And the graves were opened; and many bodies of the saints who had fallen asleep were raised; and coming out of the graves after the His resurrection, they went into the holy city and appeared unto many. (54) Now when the centurion and those with him who were guarding Jesus saw the earthquake and the things that had happened, they feared greatly saying, "Truly this was the Son of God!" *Luke 14:27*—And anyone who does not carry his cross and follow me cannot be my disciple.

Romans 5:8—But God demonstrates His own love toward us, in that while we were still sinners, Christ died for us. *1 Corinthians 1:18*—For the message of the cross is foolishness to those who are perishing, but to us who are being saved it is the power of God.

Ephesians 2:14-16—For He himself is our peace, who has made the two one and has destroyed the barrier, the dividing wall of hostility, by abolishing in His flesh the law with its commandments and regulations. His purpose was to create in Himself one new man out of two, thus making peace. And in this one body to reconcile both of them to God through the cross, by which He put to death their hostility. *Philippians 3:17-19*—Join with others in following my example, brothers, and take note of those who live according to the pattern we gave you. For as I have often told you before and now say again even with tears many live as enemies of the cross of Christ. Their destiny is destruction, their God is their stomach, and their glory is in their shame. Their mind is on earthly things. *Hebrew 12:2*—Let us fix our eyes on Jesus, the author and prefecture of our faith, who for the joy set before Him endured the cross, scorning its shame, and sat down at the right hand of the throne of God.

Walmart isn't the only saving place!

Psalm 118:22—The stone which builders rejected has become the chief cornerstone.

Isaiah 28:16—"Behold, I lay in Zion a stone for a foundation, a tried stone, a precious cornerstone, a sure foundation; Whoever believes will not act hastily.

Matthew 16:18—Jesus said, "And I say to you that you are Peter, and on this rock I will build *my* church, and the gates of Hades shall not prevail against it. [*Ephesians 2:19, 20*].

Matthew 21:42—Jesus said to them, "Did you never read in the Scriptures: *'The stone which the builders rejected has become the chief cornerstone. This was the Lord's doing, and it is marvelous in our eyes* . . . . [*Mark 12:10, Luke 20:17*]. *Acts 2:47*— . . . . and the Lord added to the church daily those being saved. *Acts 4:10-12*—" Let it be known to you all, and to all the people of Israel, that by the name of Jesus Christ of Nazareth, whom you crucified, whom God raised from the dead, by Him this man stands here before you whole. This is the 'stone which was rejected by you builders, which has become the cornerstone.' "Nor is there salvation in any other, for there is no other name under heaven given among men by which we must be saved." *Romans 9:33*—As it is written: "Behold, I lay in Zion a stumbling stone and rock of offense, and whoever believes on Him will not be put to shame." [*Romans 10:1-17; 1 Peter 2:4-10*].

For all you do, His blood's for you!

Acts 20:28— . . . . To shepherd the church of God which He purchased with His own blood.

John 19:34—Instead, one of the soldiers pierced Jesus' side with a spear, bringing a sudden flow of blood and water. *Romans 5:9*—Much more than having now been justified by His blood, we shall be saved from wrath through Him. *Ephesians 1:7*—In Him we have redemption through His blood, the forgiveness of sins, according to the riches of His grace. *Ephesians 2:13*—But now in Christ Jesus you who once were far off have been made near by the blood of Christ. *Colossians 1:19,20*—For God was pleased to have all His fullness dwell in Him (Christ) and through Him to reconcile to Himself all things, whether things on earth or things in heaven, by making peace through His blood shed on the cross.

Hebrews 10:19, 20—Therefore brethren, having boldness to enter the Holiest by the blood of Jesus, by a new and living way which He consecrated for us, through the veil, that is His flesh. *1 Peter 1:18,19*—knowing that you were not redeemed with corruptible things, like silver or gold, from your aimless conduct received by tradition from your fathers, but with the precious blood of Christ, as a lamb without blemish and without spot.

Don't wait for 6 strong men to take you to church.

Ecclesiastes 3:21—To everything there is a season. A time to be born and a time to die.

Ecclesiastes 9:5,12—For the living know that they will die; (12) For man also does not know his time: like fish taken in a cruel net, like birds caught in a snare, So the sons of men are snared in an evil time, when it falls suddenly upon them. *Acts 2:37, 38*—men and brethren what shall we do? Repent and be baptized in the name of Jesus Christ for the remission of sins; and you shall receive the gift of the Holy Spirit. (40) "Be saved from this perverse generation." (41) Then those who gladly received his word were baptized. (47) And the Lord added to the church daily those who were being saved. *Acts 11:26*—So it was that for a whole year they *assembled with the church* and taught a great many people. And the disciples were first called Christians at Antioch. *Romans 16:16*—Greet one another with a holy kiss. The churches of Christ greet you. *Ephesians 5:29*—For no one ever hated his own flesh, but nourishes and cherishes it, just as the Lord does the church. *Hebrews 10:25*—Let us not give up meeting (*assembling*) together, as some are in the habit of doing, but let us encourage one another; and all the more as you see the Day approaching.

2 Corinthians 5:17, 20—Therefore, if anyone is in Christ, he is a new creation; old things have passed away; behold all things have become new. (20) Therefore we are ambassadors for Christ, as though God were pleading through us; we implore you on Christ's behalf, be reconciled to God. *Hebrews 2:2, 3*—For if the message spoken by angels was binding, and every violation and disobedience received its just punishment, (3) how shall we escape if we ignore such a great salvation?

CHAPTER 6

Compassion is difficult to give away because it keeps coming back.

Psalm 86:15—But You, O Lord, are a God full of compassion and grace; longsuffering and abundant in mercy and truth. *Matthew 9:36*—But when He saw the multitudes, He was moved with compassion for them . . . *Matthew 15:32*—"I have compassion on the multitude because they have now continued with me three days and have nothing to eat. And I do not want to send them away hungry, lest they faint on the way. [*Mark 8:2*]

Romans 9:15—For He said to Moses, "I will have mercy on whomever I will have mercy, and I will have compassion on whomever I will have compassion." [*Exodus 33:19*]

James 5:11—Indeed we count them blessed who endure. You have heard of the perseverance of Job and seen the end intended by the Lord; that the Lord is very compassionate and merciful. *1 Peter 3:8,9*—Finally, all of you be of one mind, having compassion for one another; love as brothers, be tenderhearted, be courteous; not returning evil for evil or reviling for reviling, but on the contrary blessing, knowing that you were called to this, that you may inherit a blessing. *Jude 21, 22*—Keep yourselves in the love of our Lord Jesus Christ unto eternal life. And on some have compassion, making a distinction.

A family altar can alter a family.

Deuteronomy 6:6,7—"And these words which I command you today shall be in your heart; you shall teach them diligently to your children, and shall talk of them when you sit in your house, when you walk by the way, when you lie down, and when you rise up."

Psalm 84:3,4—Even the sparrow has found a home and the swallow a nest for herself, where she may lay her young; even Your altars, O Lords of hosts, My King and my God. Blessed are those who dwell in your house; they will still be praising you.

Proverbs 3:11, 12—My son, do not despise the chastening of the Lord, nor detest His correction. For whom the Lord loves He corrects, just as a father the son in whom he delights. *Proverbs 6:20-23*—My son, keep your father's command, and do not forsake the law of your mother. Bind them continually upon your heart; tie them around your neck. When you roam, they will lead you; when you sleep, they will keep you; and when you awake, they will speak with you. For the commandment is a lamp, and the law is the light; reproofs of instruction are the way of life. *Proverbs 22:6*—Train up a child in the way he should go, and when he is old he will not depart from it. *Ephesians 6:1-4*—Children obey your parents in the Lord, for this is right. [*Col. 3:20, 21*] "Honor your father and mother," which is the first commandment with promise; "that it may be well with you and you may live long on the earth." [*Exodus 20:12; Deut. 5:16*]. And you fathers, do not provoke your children to wrath, but bring them up in the training and admonition of the Lord.

Colossians 3:18, 19; 23, 24—(18) Wives, submit to your own husbands, as is fitting in the Lord. Husbands love your wives and do not be bitter toward them. (23) And whatever you do, do it heartily, as to the Lord and not to men, knowing that from the Lord you will receive the reward of the inheritance; for you serve the Lord Christ. *Hebrews 12:11*—No discipline seems pleasant at the time, but painful. Later on, however, it produces a harvest of righteousness and peace for those who have been trained by it.

Too blessed to be depressed/stressed.

Psalm 77:14—You are the God who does wonders; you have declared your strength among peoples. *Psalm 106:3*—Blessed are those who keep justice, and he who does righteousness at all times. *Psalm 107:6*—Then they cried out to the Lord in their trouble, and He delivered them out of their distresses. *Proverbs 12:25*—Anxiety in the heart of man causes depression, but a good word makes it glad. *Proverbs 15:13*—A merry heart makes a cheerful countenance, but by sorrow of the heart the spirit is broken. *Matthew 5:1-12*—"The Beatitudes" *1 Corinthians 10:13*—No temptation has overtaken you except such as is common to man; but God is faithful who will not allow you to be tempted beyond what you are able, but with the temptation will also make a way of escape, that you may be able to bear it. *Philippians 4:6-8*—Do not be anxious about anything, but in everything by prayer and petition, with thanksgiving, present your requests to God. And the peace of God, which transcends all understanding, will guard your hearts and your minds in Christ Jesus. *Philippians 4:13, 19*—I can do all things through Christ who strengthens me. (19) And my God shall supply your needs according to His riches in glory by Christ Jesus.

A clean conscience makes a soft pillow.

Psalm 51:10—Create in me a clean heart, O God; and renew a right spirit within me. *Acts 24:16*—This being so, I myself always strive to have a conscience without offense toward God and men. *1 Timothy 3:9*—They must keep hold of deep truths of the faith with a clear conscience. *1 Timothy 4:1,2*—The Spirit clearly says that in later times some will abandon the faith and follow deceiving spirits and things taught by demons. Such teachings come through hypocritical liars, whose consciences have been seared as with a hot iron. *Hebrews 9:14*—How much more shall the blood of Christ, who through the eternal Spirit offered Himself without spot to God, purge your conscience from dead works to serve the living God? *Hebrews 10:22*—Let us draw near with a true heart in full assurance of faith; having our hearts sprinkled from an evil conscience and our bodies washed with pure water. *1 Peter 3:15-17*—But in your hearts set apart Christ as Lord. Always be prepared to give an answer to everyone who asks you to give the reason for the hope that you have. But do this with gentleness and respect, keeping a clear conscience so that those who speak maliciously against your good behavior in Christ may be ashamed of their slander. It is better, if it is God's will, to suffer for doing good than for doing evil.

Do your best and then sleep in peace. God is Awake.

John 16:33—These things I have spoken to you, that in me you may have peace. In the world you will have tribulation; but be of good cheer, I have overcome the world.

Romans 5:1—Therefore, since we have been justified through faith, we have peace with God through our Lord Jesus Christ. *2 Corinthians 13:11*—Finally brothers, good-by. Aim for perfection, listen to my appeal, be of one mind, and live in peace. And the God of love and peace will be with you. *Ephesians 2:14, 15*—For He Himself is our peace, who made the two one and has destroyed the barrier, the dividing wall of hostility, by abolishing in His flesh the law with its commandments and regulations. His purpose was to create in Himself one new man out of the two, thus making peace. *Colossians 3:15-17*—Let the peace of Christ rule in your hearts, since as members of one body you were called to peace. And be thankful. Let the word of Christ dwell in you richly as you teach and admonish one another with all wisdom, and as you sing psalms, hymns and spiritual songs with gratitude in your hearts to God. And whatever you do, whether in word or deed, do it all in the name of the Lord Jesus, giving thanks to God the Father through Him. *James 3:18*—Peacemakers who sow in peace raise a harvest of righteousness.

Nothing else ruins the truth like stretching it.

Proverbs 19:5—A false witness will not go unpunished. And he who speaks lies will not escape. *Acts 26:25*—But he (Paul) said, "I am not mad, most noble Fetus, but speak the words of truth and reason. *Romans 1:18*—For the wrath of God is revealed from heaven against all ungodliness and unrighteousness of men who suppress the truth in unrighteousness. *Colossians 3:9, 10*—Do not lie to one another, since you have put off the old man with his deeds, and have put on the new man who is renewed in knowledge according to the image of Him . . . . *1 Corinthians 5:8*—Therefore let us keep the feast, not with old leaven, nor with the leaven of malice and wickedness, but with the unleavened bread of sincerity and truth. *James 3:14*—But if you have bitter envy and self-seeking in your hearts, do not boast and lie against the truth.

God is good all the time; All the time, God is good.

Psalm 23:6—Surely goodness and mercy shall follow me all the days of my life; and I will dwell in the house of the Lord forever. *Psalm 52:1*—Why do you boast in evil, O mighty man? The goodness of God endures continually. *Psalm 73:1*—Truly God is good to Israel, to such as are pure in heart. *Psalm 86:5*—For You, Lord, are good and ready to forgive, and abundant in mercy to all those who call upon you.

Proverbs 15:3—The eyes of the Lord are in every place, keeping watch on the evil and the good. *Matthew 5:45*—"That you may be sons of your Father in heaven; for He makes His sun rise on the evil and on the good, and sends rain on the just and on the unjust."

Acts 14:17—Nevertheless He did not leave Himself without witness, in that He did good, gave us rain from heaven and fruitful seasons, filling our hearts with food and gladness.

Romans 2:4—Or do you despise the riches of His goodness, forbearance, and longsuffering, not knowing that the goodness of God leads you to repentance? *Romans 11:22*—Therefore consider the goodness and severity of God: On those who fell, severity; but toward you, goodness, if you continue in His goodness. Otherwise you also will be cut off.

James 1:17—Every good gift and every perfect gift is from above, and comes down from the Father of lights, with whom there is no variation or shadow of turning.